United States Government Accountability Office

Report to Congressional Requesters

April 2013

EMERGENCY ALERTING

Capabilities Have Improved, but Additional Guidance and Testing Are Needed

GAO

Accountability ★ Integrity ★ Reliability

GAO-13-375

April 2013

EMERGENCY ALERTING

Capabilities Have Improved, but Additional Guidance and Testing Are Needed

Why GAO Did This Study

An effective system to alert the public during emergencies can help reduce property damage and save lives. In 2004, FEMA initiated IPAWS with the goal of integrating the nation's EAS and other public-alerting systems into a comprehensive alerting system. In 2009, GAO reported on long-standing weaknesses with EAS and FEMA's limited progress in implementing IPAWS. Subsequently, FEMA and FCC conducted the first-ever nationwide EAS test in November 2011. GAO was asked to review recent efforts to implement IPAWS and improve EAS. GAO examined: (1) how IPAWS capabilities have changed since 2009 and what barriers, if any, affect its implementation and (2) results of the nationwide EAS test and federal efforts to address identified weaknesses. GAO reviewed FEMA, FCC, and other documentation, and interviewed industry stakeholders and alerting authorities from six locations that were selected because they have public-alerting systems in addition to EAS and experienced problems during the nationwide EAS test.

What GAO Recommends

GAO recommends that FEMA work in conjunction with FCC to establish guidance for states to fully implement and test IPAWS components and implement a strategy for regular nationwide EAS testing. In response, the Department of Homeland Security (DHS) concurred with GAO's recommendations and provided examples of actions aimed at addressing the recommendations. DHS, FCC, and the Department of Commerce also provided technical comments, which have been incorporated as appropriate.

View GAO-13-375. For more information, contact Mark Goldstein at (202) 512-2834 or goldsteinm@gao.gov

What GAO Found

Since 2009, the Federal Emergency Management Agency (FEMA) has taken actions to improve the capabilities of the Integrated Public Alert and Warning System (IPAWS) and to increase federal, state, and local capabilities to alert the public, but barriers remain to fully implementing an integrated system. Specifically, IPAWS has the capability to receive and authenticate Internet-based alerts from federal, state, and local public authorities and disseminate them to the public through multiple systems. For example, since January 2012, public-alerting authorities can disseminate Emergency Alert System (EAS) messages through IPAWS to television and radio stations. Beginning in April 2012, alerting authorities have used IPAWS to transmit alerts via the Commercial Mobile Alert System interface to disseminate text-like messages to mobile phones. FEMA also adopted alert standards and increased coordination efforts with multiple stakeholders. Although FEMA has taken important steps to advance an integrated system, state and local alerting authorities we contacted cited a need for more guidance from FEMA on how to integrate and test IPAWS capabilities with their existing alerting systems. For example, an official with a state alerting authority said that additional guidance from FEMA is needed to determine what systems and policies should be put in place before integrating and testing IPAWS with other public alerting systems in the state's 128 counties and cities. In the absence of sufficient guidance from FEMA, states we contacted are reluctant to fully implement IPAWS. This reluctance decreases the capability for an integrated, interoperable, and nationwide alerting system.

The Federal Communications Commission (FCC) required all EAS participants (e.g., broadcast radio and television, cable operators, satellite radio and television service providers, and wireline video-service providers) to submit a report to FCC by December 27, 2011, on the results of the nationwide EAS test. As of January 2013, 61 percent of broadcasters and cable operators had submitted the required report. Of those, 82 percent reported receiving the nationwide test alert, and 61 percent reported successfully retransmitting the alert to other stations, as required. Broadcasters' and cable operators' reception of the alert varied by state, from 6 percent in Oregon to 100 percent in Delaware. Key reasons for reception or retransmission difficulties included poor audio quality, outdated broadcaster-monitoring assignments, and equipment failure. For example, poor audio quality of the test alert resulted in some broadcasters' receiving a garbled and degraded audio message and others' receiving a duplicate alert that caused equipment to malfunction. According to FEMA officials, the poor audio quality is being addressed, in part, with the deployment of a dedicated satellite network that will become fully operational by fall 2013. However, at the time of our review, FEMA and FCC had taken few steps to address other problems identified in the nationwide test. Furthermore, while FCC rules call for periodic nationwide EAS testing, it is uncertain when the next test will occur. Without a strategy for regular nationwide testing of the relay distribution system, including developing milestones and timeframes and reporting on after-action plans, there is no assurance that EAS would work as intended should the President need to activate it to communicate with the American people.

Contents

Figures

Abbreviations

AMBER	America's Missing Broadcast Emergency Response
CAP	Common Alerting Protocol
CMAS	Commercial Mobile Alert System
DHS	Department of Homeland Security
EAS	Emergency Alert System
FCC	Federal Communications Commission
FEMA	Federal Emergency Management Agency
HazCollect	All Hazards Emergency Message Collection System
IPAWS	Integrated Public Alert and Warning System
NEMA	National Emergency Management Association
NOAA	National Oceanic and Atmospheric Administration
PEP	primary entry point
WARN Act	Warning, Alert, Response, Network Act

United States Government Accountability Office
Washington, DC 20548

April 24, 2013

The Honorable Bill Shuster
Chairman
Committee on Transportation and Infrastructure
House of Representatives

The Honorable Lou Barletta
Chairman
The Honorable Eleanor Holmes Norton
Ranking Member
Subcommittee on Economic Development, Public Buildings, and
   Emergency Management
Committee on Transportation and Infrastructure
House of Representatives

The Honorable Jeff Denham
House of Representatives

Effective public emergency alerts via various telecommunications modes are critical in major events such as natural disaster, terrorist attack, or war. A reliable and comprehensive system to alert Americans during emergencies can help save lives and reduce damages and hardship. The Emergency Alert System (EAS) is a national public warning system that requires broadcasters, cable operators, and other communications service providers to provide the President with communications capability to address the American people during a national emergency.

Although EAS was originally designed to alert the public via radios and televisions, in June 2006, an executive order directed the Department of Homeland Security (DHS) to modernize the nation's public-alerting systems to ensure the capability of distributing alerts though a variety of telecommunications devices beyond broadcast media. The Federal Emergency Management Agency (FEMA) within DHS is responsible for modernizing EAS and implementing the Integrated Public Alert and Warning System (IPAWS), which is intended to integrate EAS and other public-alerting systems into a larger network to form a comprehensive public-alerting system. In September 2009, we reported that EAS exhibited long-standing weaknesses that limit its effectiveness and that

FEMA had made little progress in implementing IPAWS.[1] In November 2011, FEMA, in conjunction with the Federal Communications Commission (FCC), conducted the first-ever nationwide test of EAS, which revealed that some portions of the system did not work as intended. Building on our previous work, you asked us to provide information on recent efforts to implement IPAWS and improve EAS. We examined (1) how the capabilities of IPAWS have changed since 2009 and what barriers, if any, are affecting its implementation and (2) the results of the nationwide EAS test and federal efforts under way to address identified weaknesses.

To meet these objectives, we examined federal agency data and reports since 2009, including FEMA's inventory and evaluation of public-alerting systems; the IPAWS program management plan; nationwide EAS test data and preliminary reports; and various agency orders and rules. To determine the reliability of the data used in this report, we reviewed relevant documentation and interviewed agency officials about their processes for reviewing the data and ensuring their accuracy. We found the agency data were sufficiently reliable for the purposes of our review. We met with officials from FCC, FEMA, DHS, and the National Oceanic and Atmospheric Administration (NOAA) to understand the agencies' progress in implementing IPAWS and efforts to address weaknesses identified from the nationwide EAS test. For both objectives, we also met with representatives from industry trade groups, including radio and television broadcasters, cable operators, and wireless service providers, and an organization representing individuals with disabilities. In six locations—California, Kentucky, Oklahoma, Oregon, Wisconsin, and the District of Columbia—we interviewed state and local alerting authorities, state emergency-communication-committee chairs, the state broadcasters association, and selected local broadcasters. We selected these states and the District of Columbia because, among other things, they have additional public-alerting systems other than EAS, and some have the ability to provide alerts for individuals with disabilities and limited English. The selected states also experienced problems during the nationwide EAS test. Results from our review of the selected states and localities are not generalizable.

---

[1]GAO, *Emergency Preparedness: Improved Planning and Coordination Necessary for Modernization and Integration of Public Alert and Warning System*, GAO-09-834 (Washington, D.C.: Sept. 9, 2009).

We conducted this performance audit from June 2012 through April 2013, in accordance with generally accepted government auditing standards. Those standards require that we plan and perform the audit to obtain sufficient, appropriate evidence to provide a reasonable basis for our findings and conclusions based on our audit objectives. We believe that the evidence obtained provides a reasonable basis for our findings and conclusions based on our audit objectives. A more detailed discussion of our objectives, scope, and methodology appears in appendix I.

Background

EAS serves as the nation's primary alerting system. It provides the President the capability to issue alerts and communicate to the public in response to emergencies. It was built on a structure conceived in the 1950s when over-the-air broadcasting was the best-available technology for widely disseminating emergency alerts. EAS has been upgraded numerous times since then, including in 2005 to include digital broadcast television as well as satellite radio and television. EAS was further expanded to include Internet-protocol-based television in 2007.

FEMA, in partnership with FCC and NOAA, is responsible for operating and maintaining EAS at the federal level. NOAA's National Weather Service and state and local alerting authorities, in conjunction with local radio and television stations, can also use EAS to disseminate emergency messages, including weather warnings, America's Missing: Broadcast Emergency Response (AMBER) Alerts,[2] and other public emergency communications, targeted to specific regional and local areas and independent from a presidential alert.

Presidential EAS alerts, also known as national-level alerts, use a hierarchical broadcast-based distribution system to relay emergency messages, as shown in figure 1. As the entry point for national-level EAS messages, FEMA is responsible for distributing such alerts to National Primary stations, often referred to as primary entry point (PEP) stations.[3] Broadcasts of national-level alerts are relayed by the PEP stations across

---

[2]The AMBER Alert Program is a voluntary collaboration among law-enforcement agencies, broadcasters, transportation agencies, and the wireless industry to activate an urgent bulletin in the most serious child-abduction cases.

[3]PEP stations are usually private or commercial radio stations, but FEMA also designated some satellite providers as PEP stations, such as SiriusXM Satellite and National Public Radio's Satellite System News Advisory Channel.

the country to radio and television stations that rebroadcast the audio and visual message to other broadcast stations, cable systems, and other EAS participants[4] until all participants have been alerted. This retransmission of alerts from EAS participant to EAS participant is commonly referred to as a "daisy chain" distribution system.

---

[4]EAS participants are entities required under FCC rules to comply with EAS rules and include radio and television broadcast stations, wired and wireless cable television systems, direct broadcast satellite service providers, satellite digital audio radio service providers, and wireline video systems. 47 C.F.R. § 11.2 (d).

GAO-13-375 Emergency Alerting Capabilities

Figure 1: Flowchart for National-Level Alerts

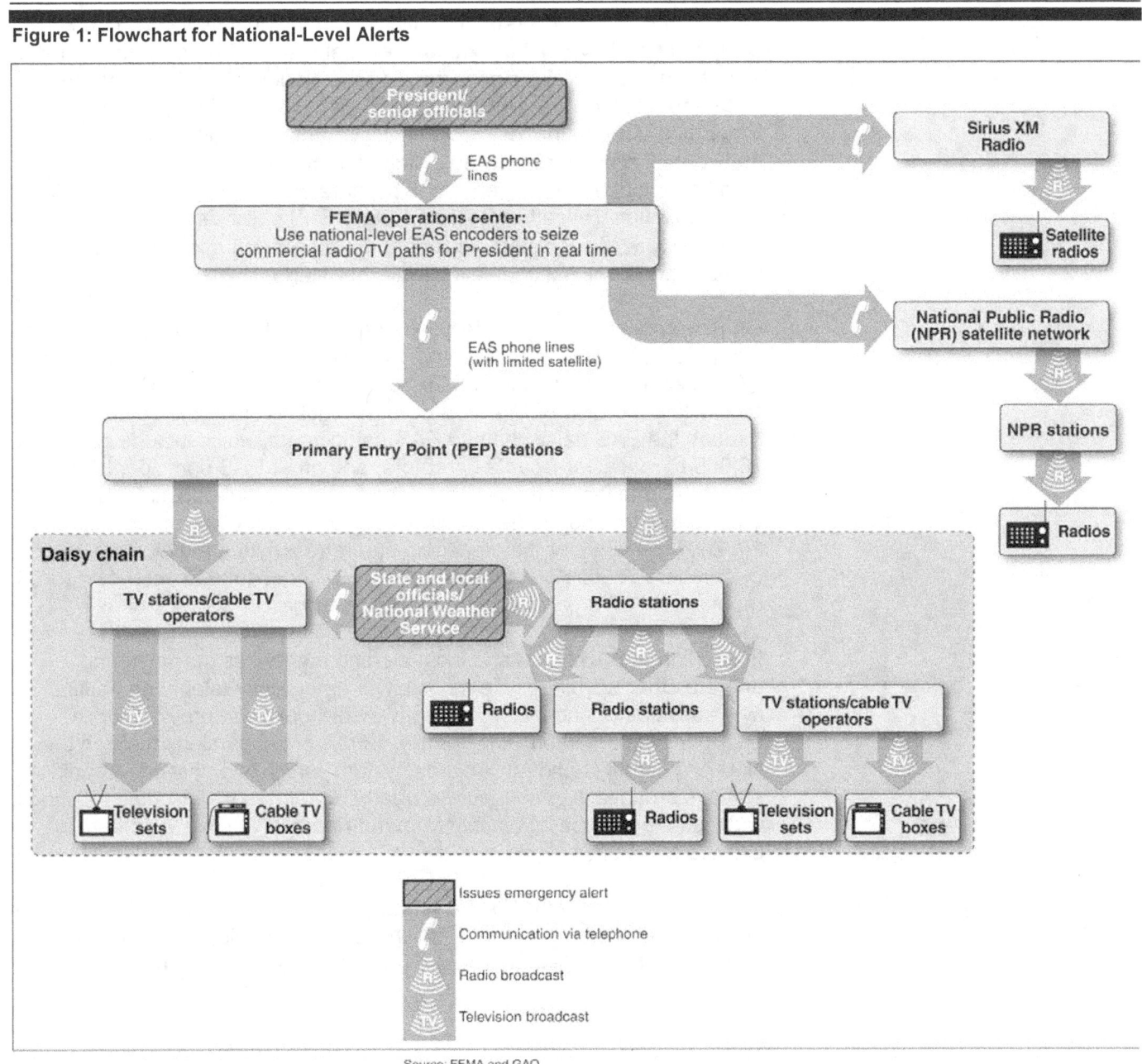

Source: FEMA and GAO.

While FEMA is responsible for administering EAS at the national-level, FCC adopts, administers, and enforces rules governing EAS and the EAS

GAO-13-375 Emergency Alerting Capabilities

participants. FCC rules require EAS participants to install FCC-certified equipment and transmit all national-level alerts; EAS participants can also voluntarily transmit alerts generated by the National Weather Service or state and local alerting authorities. EAS participants, through their State Emergency Communications Committee,[5] may maintain state EAS plans that contain procedures for the distribution of national-level alerts as well as other voluntary alerts generated by state and local alerting authorities and the National Weather Service.[6] State EAS plans describe the EAS relay network of each state, including the monitoring assignments of EAS participants for all national-level and other alerts.

On November 9, 2011, FEMA conducted the first-ever nationwide test of the national-level EAS in response to our prior reports noting the lack of EAS testing. FEMA conducted the test in conjunction with FCC. In conducting the test, FEMA initiated a national-level alert to be distributed through the EAS daisy chain to EAS participants, which include about 26,000 broadcasters, cable operators, and other EAS participants. To obtain information on the results of the test, FCC directed all EAS participants to report either electronically or via paper report by December 27, 2011, on whether they received and retransmitted the alert. Although December 27, 2011, was the deadline, FCC continued to accept paper reports from EAS participants past the deadline.

In addition to EAS, state and local alerting authorities may own and operate other warning systems, such as emergency telephone notification systems, sirens, and electronic highway billboards, to provide public emergency information. Additionally, NOAA provides alerts through the NOAA Weather Radio All Hazards system, which is a network of radio stations broadcasting continuous weather information, including warnings, watches, and forecasts directly from the nearest National Weather Service office.

In 2004, FEMA initiated IPAWS to integrate EAS and other public-alerting systems into a larger, more comprehensive public-alerting system. In June 2006, the President issued Executive Order No. 13407, entitled

---

[5]State Emergency Communications Committees are groups in each state that are comprised of radio and television broadcasters, cable companies, and state alerting authorities.

[6]47 C.F.R. § 11.21.

Public Alert and Warning System, adopting a policy that the United States have a comprehensive, integrated alerting system. The order directs the Secretary of Homeland Security to "ensure an orderly and effective transition" from current capabilities to a more coordinated and integrated system and details the responsibilities of the Secretary in meeting the President's directive.[7] As shown in table 1, the executive order established 10 responsibilities for the Secretary of Homeland Security. It is FEMA's intention that IPAWS be the programmatic mechanism to carry out the executive order.

Table 1: Responsibilities of the Secretary of Homeland Security to Form a Comprehensive Public-Alerting System under Executive Order No. 13407 (2006)

Responsibilities
1. Inventory, evaluate, and assess the capabilities and integration with the public alert and warning system of federal, state, territorial, tribal, and local public-alert and warning resources.
2. Establish or adopt, as appropriate, common alerting and warning protocols, standards, terminology, and operating procedures for the public-alert and warning system to enable interoperability and the secure delivery of coordinated messages to the American people through as many communication pathways as practicable, taking into account FCC rules, as provided by law.
3. Ensure the capability to adapt the distribution and content of communications based on geographic location, risks, or personal user preferences, as appropriate.
4. Include in the public-alert and warning system the capability to alert and warn all Americans, including those with disabilities and those without an understanding of the English language.
5. Through cooperation with the owners and operators of communication facilities, maintain, protect, and if necessary, restore communication facilities and capabilities necessary for the public-alert and warning system.
6. Ensure the conduct of training, tests, and exercises for the public-alert and warning system.
7. Ensure the conduct of public education efforts.
8. Consult, coordinate, and cooperate with the private sector, including communications media organizations, and federal, state, territorial, tribal, and local governmental authorities, including emergency response providers, as appropriate.
9. Administer the EAS as a critical component of the public-alert and warning system.
10. Ensure that under all conditions the President of the United States can alert and warn the American people.

Source: Executive Order No. 13407.

---

[7]Exec. Order No. 13407, 71 Fed. Reg. 36,975.

In addition, in 2006, the Warning, Alert, Response Network Act (WARN Act)[8] was enacted, which required FCC to adopt relevant technical standards, protocols, procedures, and other technical requirements to enable commercial mobile service providers (e.g., wireless providers) to issue emergency alerts.[9] The act required FCC to establish an advisory panel called the Commercial Mobile Service Alert Advisory Committee to recommend technical specifications and protocols to govern wireless service providers participation in emergency alerting.[10] In 2008, following public notice and opportunity for public comment as required by the Administrative Procedure Act,[11] FCC adopted many of the committee's recommendations for wireless providers to transmit alerts and began developing the Commercial Mobile Alert System (CMAS),[12] in conjunction with FEMA.[13]

We previously reported several factors that limited EAS effectiveness and delayed IPAWS implementation.[14] For example, in 2009, we reported that a lack of redundancy and testing and gaps in coverage, including capabilities to reach individuals with disabilities and non-English speakers, significantly limited EAS reliability and efficiency. We also reported in 2009 that IPAWS program implementation had stalled, as state and local governments were forging ahead with their own alerting systems. We made several recommendations to FEMA to improve program management and enhance transparency about the progress

---

[8]The WARN Act was enacted as title VI of the Security and Accountability for Every Port Act, Pub. L. No. 109-347, § 602, 120 Stat. 1,884, 1,936 (2006), codified at 47 U.S.C. ch. 11.

[9]47 U.S.C. § 1201.

[10]47 U.S.C. § 1202.

[11]5 U.S.C. § 553(c).

[12]FCC recently released an order amending Part 10 of the FCC rules to change references from "Commercial Mobile Alert System" and "CMAS" to "Wireless Emergency Alerts" and "WEA." *In the Matter of Commercial Mobile Alert System*, PS Docket No. 07-287, (PSHSB, Feb. 25, 2013).

[13]*In the Matter of the Commercial Mobile Alert System,* 23 FCC Rcd. 6144 (2008), *reconsidered, clarified and corrected,* 23 FCC Rcd. 11,669 (2008), with *errata,* 23 FCC Rcd.12,561 (2008)

[14]GAO-09-834 and GAO, *Emergency Preparedness: Current Emergency Alert System Has Limitations, and Development of a New Integrated System Will Be Challenging,* GAO-07-411 (Washington, D.C.: Mar. 30, 2007).

toward achieving an integrated public-alerting system. FEMA implemented all our recommendations, including periodically reporting on the status of implementing IPAWS to congressional committees and subcommittees.[15]

IPAWS Capabilities Have Improved, but Barriers to Implementation Exist

FEMA has Increased Federal, State, and Local Alerting Capabilities Since 2009

Since we reported on these issues in 2009, FEMA has taken actions to improve IPAWS capabilities. In particular, FEMA implemented a federal alert aggregator in 2010, called the IPAWS Open Platform for Emergency Networks,[16] which has increased alerting capabilities for authorities at the federal, state, and local level.[17] The alert aggregator is capable of receiving and authenticating alerts from public-alerting authorities and routing them to various public-alerting systems. As of January 2013, 93 public-alerting authorities,[18] including those in at least 35 states, have gone through the necessary authentication steps with FEMA to use IPAWS and an additional 110 alerting authorities have applications in process.[19] Authorized public-alerting authorities may use IPAWS-compatible software to compose and transmit alerts via the Internet to the

---

[15]Information on the specific actions FEMA took to implement our recommendations is available at http://www.gao.gov/products/GAO-09-834.

[16]Throughout this report, we refer to IPAWS Open Platform for Emergency Networks simply as IPAWS.

[17]U.S. territories and tribal governments can also use the federal aggregator for public alerting.

[18]According to a survey FEMA conducted from January 2010 through December 2011, more than 3,300 public-alerting authorities existed in the United States at that time.

[19]FEMA requires alerting authorities to take specific steps to become authorized alert originators. A federal, state, local, tr bal or territorial alerting authority can become an authorized alert originator by (1) selecting IPAWS compatible software, (2) applying for a memorandum of agreement with FEMA, (3) applying for public-alerting permissions, and (4) completing IPAWS web-based training. Use of IPAWS for federal, state, and local authorities is voluntary, and there is no cost to send messages through IPAWS, although there may be costs associated with acquiring IPAWS-compatible software.

alert aggregator using a common standard, called the Common Alerting Protocol (CAP).[20] According to FEMA, once the alert aggregator verifies the credentials of the message, an alert may be distributed to the public through multiple alerting systems,[21] which make up the components of IPAWS, as follows:

- **EAS.** As of January 2012, public-alerting authorities can disseminate CAP-formatted EAS alerts through the alert aggregator to television and radio stations.[22] As of June 30, 2012, FCC required EAS participants (i.e., radio and television broadcasters, cable operators) to have in place CAP-compatible equipment and monitor the IPAWS EAS feed so they can retrieve and retransmit Internet-based EAS alerts. State and local alerting authorities' use of IPAWS to send EAS alerts is voluntary and as of January 2013, no public-alerting authorities had used IPAWS to send an EAS alert. However, according to FEMA, state and local alerting authorities had sent 81 EAS test messages via the alert aggregator between January 2012 and January 2013.

- **All-Hazards Emergency Message Collection System (HazCollect).** NOAA's HazCollect system connected to IPAWS in September 2012, and enables federal, state, and local alerting authorities to send non-weather emergency messages through IPAWS to the National Weather Service's alerting systems, including NOAA Weather Radio's nationwide network of radio stations.[23] Examples of non-weather emergency message events can include wildfires, hazardous materials releases, terrorist incidents, AMBER alerts, and public

---

[20]CAP is an open, non-proprietary digital message format that is compatible with multiple applications and telecommunications methods.

[21]The various alerting systems either receive a pushed message—meaning data is sent by the server to the user—or poll for a message from the alert aggregator—meaning data is pulled from the server by the user.

[22]According to FEMA, the IPAWS EAS Atom Feed came online on September 2011. FEMA began processing applications for IPAWS public alerting authorities in June 2011 and FEMA began posting weekly tests to the IPAWS EAS Internet feed in January 2012. To access the IPAWS EAS feed, public-alerting authorities need Internet connectivity, appropriate equipment (CAP EAS Encoder/Decoder) and software, and must complete FEMA's authentication steps to become an authorized user of IPAWS.

[23]Other National Weather Service dissemination systems include the NOAA Weather Wire Service, Emergency Managers Weather Information Network, National Weather Service Websites, Internet feeds, and others.

health emergencies. According to FEMA, EAS participants generally monitor the NOAA Weather Radio directly for emergency alerts. As a result, IPAWS with HazCollect provides an alternate means for EAS participants to receive non-weather alerts from local alerting authorities, increasing the number of alerting channels and enhancing the likelihood that the public will receive timely alerts. According to FEMA, 22 NOAA Weather Radio messages had been sent via the alert aggregator as of January 2013.

- **CMAS.** Starting in April 2012, public-alerting authorities can use IPAWS to transmit alerts via the CMAS interface to disseminate mobile alerts, which are geo-targeted, text-like messages to mobile phones.[24] These alerts are limited to 90 characters and emit a unique ring tone and vibration cadence, which is intended to, among other things, improve capabilities for notifying individuals with disabilities during an emergency. This new capability is designed to relay presidential (or national-level), AMBER, and imminent threat alerts to mobile phones using cell technology that is not subject to the congestion typically experienced on wireless networks during times of emergency.[25] Most imminent threat alerts are issued by the National Weather Service, which began sending severe weather-related alerts to all regions of the country in June 2012. According to FEMA, as of January 2013, the National Weather Service had sent 2,667 weather alerts via CMAS. An additional 3 imminent threat alerts had been sent from one state related to Hurricane Sandy and 17 AMBER alerts had been sent from the National Center for Missing and Exploited Children.[26] While CMAS became operational in April 2012, participation by wireless carriers is optional under the WARN Act.[27]

---

[24]CMAS is a partnership between FEMA, FCC, and wireless carriers to enhance public safety. The rules for CMAS are published at 47 C.F.R. ch. I, subchapter A, pt.10. In December 2009, FEMA formally adopted the CMAS Interface Specification, which defined the interface between the federal alert aggregator gateway and the commercial service provider gateways. This initiated a 28-month period during which participating commercial mobile service providers needed to develop, test, and deploy their portion of CMAS.

[25]Cell phone users may opt out of receiving imminent threat and AMBER alerts, but may not opt out of receiving presidential alerts.

[26]The National Center for Missing and Exploited Children is a nonprofit organization whose mission is to serve as the nation's resource on the issues of missing and sexually exploited children.

[27]47 U.S.C. §1201 (b)(2).

Nevertheless, according to CTIA—The Wireless Association, all of the major wireless carriers have agreed to participate.[28] Some carriers may still be rolling out CMAS capabilities and not all cell phones are yet capable of receiving alerts, according to CTIA. Some state and local alerting authorities we contacted raised concerns about the degree of granularity for geo-targeting these alerts, which we discuss later in this report.

- **Internet services.** As of September 2012, Internet web services (e.g., Google Public Alerts) and software application developers can retrieve and redistribute IPAWS alerts to the public through their own services, such as websites, mobile phone applications, email, and text messaging. To do so, an alert redistribution service must complete a memorandum of agreement with FEMA, which then grants them access to the IPAWS Public Alerts Feed from the alert aggregator.

- **State and local alerting systems.** According to FEMA, existing state or locally owned and operated public-alerting systems—such as sirens and emergency telephone notification systems—may also be configured to receive alerts from IPAWS.

FEMA views the new capabilities for public-alerting authorities to distribute CAP-formatted messages through the federal alert aggregator as an added capability, not a replacement, to the traditional national-level alert (i.e., EAS daisy chain relay distribution system). As a result, FEMA officials said they anticipate maintaining both systems into the foreseeable future as parallel alerting systems, as shown in figure 2. FEMA officials also told us that discussions with the White House are ongoing to determine use of IPAWS during a presidential alert; however, at the time of our report, FEMA officials said a national-level alert would not be disseminated through the federal alert aggregator.[29]

---

[28]CTIA is an international non-profit organization that represents the wireless communications industry. Membership in the association includes wireless carriers and their suppliers, as well as providers and manufacturers of wireless data services and products.

[29]In addition, FEMA officials said there are additional challenges to sending a national-level alert directly to EAS participant stations through both IPAWS and the traditional system. Specifically, uncertainty exists regarding technical malfunctions that could occur with equipment if EAS participant stations simultaneously received an alert both through the PEP stations via the traditional daisy chain and the alert aggregator. FEMA officials said that until these technical issues are resolved, FEMA would not distribute a CAP-formatted national-level alert to EAS participant stations through IPAWS.

Figure 2: National-Level EAS and Current IPAWS Architecture

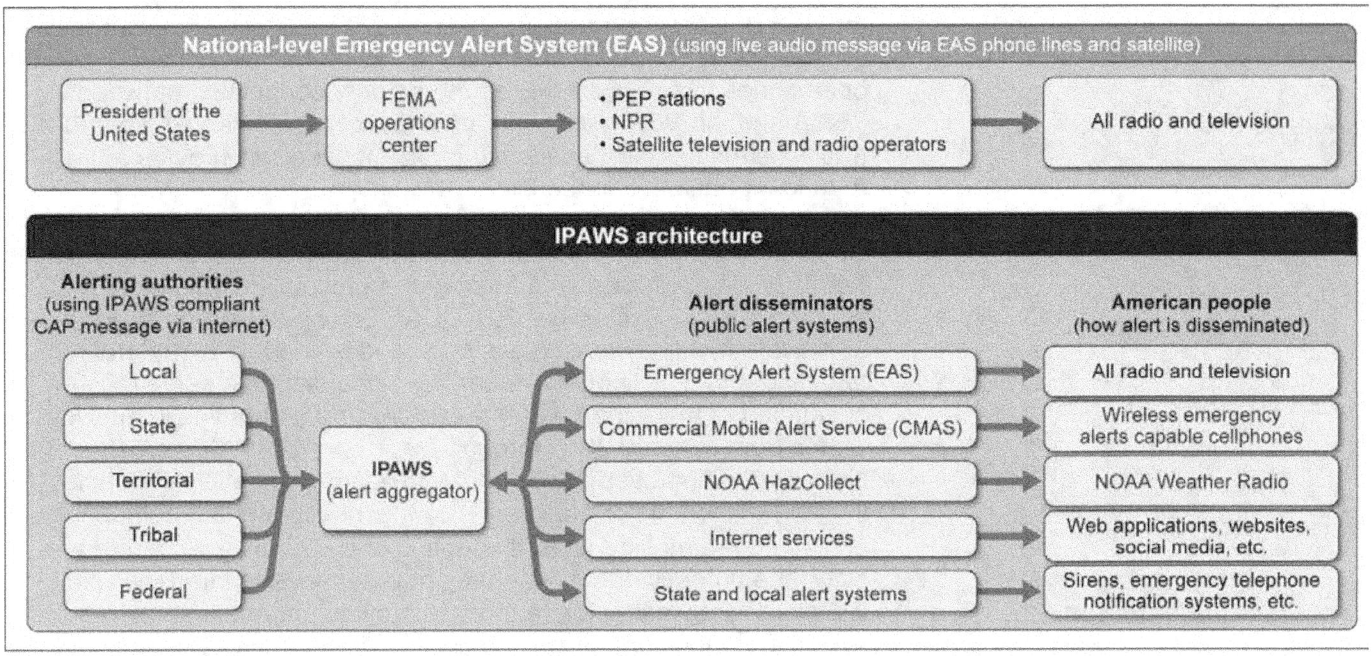

National-level Emergency Alert System (EAS) (using live audio message via EAS phone lines and satellite)

President of the United States → FEMA operations center → • PEP stations • NPR • Satellite television and radio operators → All radio and television

IPAWS architecture

Alerting authorities (using IPAWS compliant CAP message via internet)
- Local
- State
- Territorial
- Tribal
- Federal

IPAWS (alert aggregator)

Alert disseminators (public alert systems)
- Emergency Alert System (EAS)
- Commercial Mobile Alert Service (CMAS)
- NOAA HazCollect
- Internet services
- State and local alert systems

American people (how alert is disseminated)
- All radio and television
- Wireless emergency alerts capable cellphones
- NOAA Weather Radio
- Web applications, websites, social media, etc.
- Sirens, emergency telephone notification systems, etc.

Sources: FEMA and GAO.

In addition to creating the alert aggregator, FEMA has taken other actions to implement the IPAWS program and address directives in Executive Order No. 13407. Specific examples include:

- **Expanded and modernized PEP stations.** To increase direct coverage of a presidential alert and address executive order directives to augment infrastructure for the public alert and warning system, FEMA has expanded the number of PEP stations from 34 in 2009 (directly covering about 67 percent of the American population) to 65 in 2012 (directly covering about 85 percent of the American population), according to FEMA officials. FEMA plans to further expand and modernize this network, with the goal of having a total of 77 PEP stations operational by fall 2013, providing direct coverage to over 90 percent of the American population.[30] FEMA officials said they have also added satellite connectivity in 50 PEP stations, with the goal of a fully operational, dedicated PEP satellite network to all 77 stations by fall 2013. According to FEMA officials, once operational, this network will be the primary connection between FEMA and the PEP stations in the event of a presidential alert; the traditional telephone-based distribution network will provide a redundant backup connection.

- **Adopted CAP standard.** To address directives in the executive order that DHS develop alert standards and protocols, FEMA formally adopted CAP in September 2010. CAP can be used as a single input to activate multiple warning systems, and is capable of geographic targeting and multilingual messaging. According to a survey FEMA conducted of more than 3,300 public-alerting authorities in the United States from January 2010 through December 2011, 64 percent of the sites responding used CAP and had IPAWS-compatible Products in place at the time of the survey.[31] Most public-alerting authorities we contacted are moving toward adoption of CAP; however, some are still in the process of implementing new software to interface with IPAWS or are waiting for vendors to provide upgrades to their existing systems. In addition, representatives from the broadcast industry told us, based on experience, that the vast majority of broadcasters are able to receive CAP-formatted alerts, as required by FCC rules.

- **Developed IPAWS training and webinars.** Executive Order No. 13407 directs DHS to conduct training for the public alert and warning system. To address this directive, FEMA developed an independent training course for alerting authorities on IPAWS capabilities, which has been available online since December 2011. The goal of the course is to provide public-alerting authorities with increased awareness of the benefits of using IPAWS for public warnings; skills to draft more appropriate, effective, and accessible warning messages; and best practices in the effective use of CAP to reach all

---

[30]Although roughly 10 percent of the population will not be covered by a PEP station, the public may also be reached by other EAS participants (e.g., satellite TV providers). Information on the specific areas of the country that have PEP station coverage is available at http://www.fema.gov/primary-entry-point-stations.

[31]FEMA, *IPAWS Inventory and Evaluation Assessment Report*, December 2011. See appendix I for a description of the survey used to produce the inventory.

members of their communities. In addition, the IPAWS program office conducts monthly webinars for developers and alerting practitioners.

- **Conducted outreach to partners.** Since 2009, the IPAWS program office has made efforts to improve communication and outreach to stakeholders at all levels, according to FEMA officials. Executive Order No. 13407 directs FEMA to consult, coordinate, and cooperate with the private sector, as well as provide public education on IPAWS. Some government and private stakeholders told us that FEMA's communication and coordination efforts have improved significantly since 2009, although improvements could still be made, especially in educating the public, as discussed below. According to FEMA officials, the IPAWS program office works to engage federal entities; state, local, tribal, and territorial alerting authorities; private sector industry; non-profit and advocacy groups; and the American people through working groups and roundtables, conferences, demonstrations, trainings and webinars, Congressional briefings, and the IPAWS Web site, among other mechanisms.

For a complete list of actions FEMA has taken to address Executive Order No. 13407, see appendix II.

Barriers Remain to Fully Implementing and Using IPAWS

Although FEMA has taken important steps to advance an integrated alerting system, barriers exist that may impede IPAWS implementation at the state and local level. Specifically, public-alerting authorities we contacted, as well as representatives from national trade industry groups, identified five main barriers at the state and local level. These barriers include (1) insufficient guidance on how states should fully implement IPAWS; (2) inability of state and local alerting authorities to test all IPAWS components; (3) CMAS geo-targeting and character limitations; (4) inadequate public outreach on IPAWS capabilities; and (5) limited resources at the federal, state, and local level to fully implement IPAWS.

- **Insufficient guidance to fully implement IPAWS.** While most state and local alerting authorities we contacted, including representatives from the National Emergency Management Association,[32] said they

---

[32]The National Emergency Management Association (NEMA) is a non-partisan, non-profit association dedicated to enhancing public safety by improving the nation's ability to prepare for, respond to, and recover from all emergencies, disasters, and threats to our nation's security. NEMA is the professional association of and for emergency management directors from all 50 states, 8 U.S. territories, and the District of Columbia.

are moving toward implementing IPAWS, some are reluctant to fully implement the system, citing a need for more information and additional guidance from FEMA.[33] Specifically, while current IPAWS training exists to instruct public-alerting authorities on, among other things, how to draft an appropriate IPAWS alert, state and local alerting authorities we contacted said additional guidance is needed on integrating and operating IPAWS with existing state and local public-alerting systems in their states. For example, officials in one state said that while they are prepared to use IPAWS, they have not yet integrated their state and local alerting systems with IPAWS, citing a need for additional guidance from FEMA and communication within the state to determine what systems and policies should be put in place to integrate IPAWS with public-alerting systems in the state's 128 counties and cities. Although Executive Order No. 13407 directs DHS to ensure interoperability and the delivery of coordinated public messages through multiple communication pathways, we found that none of our selected states had yet integrated their alerting systems with IPAWS for state or local level alerting, although according to FEMA, the alerting authorities had gone through the necessary steps to become authenticated IPAWS originators. Since IPAWS is still in the early stages of its deployment, officials said that there are no examples of how to effectively implement IPAWS at the state and local level. In commenting on a draft of this report, FEMA officials noted that they are involved in efforts to conduct case studies with public-alerting authorities in Nebraska and Nevada to provide examples of effectively implementing IPAWS at the state level. FEMA officials said they are working with state and local alerting authorities as well as system developers and vendors, to address some notable challenges related to implementing IPAWS, including how states can manage IPAWS capabilities within their respective states. Nevertheless, in the absence of additional FEMA guidance, some states are reluctant to fully implement IPAWS, a reluctance that decreases the capability for an integrated, interoperable, and nationwide alerting system.

- **Inability of state and local alerting authorities to test all IPAWS components.** Some officials from state and local alerting authorities we contacted were also reluctant to use IPAWS because procedures

---

[33]According to FEMA, system developers and vendors conduct the technical integration of the alerting systems. FEMA is continuing to provide ongoing support to the developer community via webinars and published guides.

for them to test all IPAWS components do not exist. As a result, they cannot assess the system's reliability or effectiveness. For example, while there are procedures for public-alerting authorities to test EAS alerts via IPAWS, currently, the only way state and local alerting authorities could potentially test CMAS is to send a live alert, which is not permissible under FCC rules. Although FCC's CMAS rules allow FEMA to test the system, according to FCC officials, these testing procedures do not extend to state and local alerting authorities that wish to use CMAS. As a result, FEMA officials told us they are working with FCC and other stakeholders to elevate the importance of clarifying rules for public-alerting partners, especially as it relates to how state and local alerting authorities can test mobile alerts using IPAWS. Although FCC officials told us in January 2013 that it was premature to review the CMAS rules, FCC subsequently said it plans to have one of its federal advisory committees, the Communications Security, Reliability and Interoperability Council, review the CMAS rules, including those related to testing procedures.[34] However, until FEMA and FCC develop procedures for state and local alerting authorities to test all IPAWS components, the state and local authorities have no assurances that emergency alerts will be effectively distributed and therefore may be unlikely to use the untested IPAWS components. In commenting on a draft of this report, FCC noted that while state and local alerting authorities have expressed a desire to test CMAS capabilities, wireless industry stakeholders have consistently raised concerns about their doing so.

- **CMAS geo-targeting and character limitations.**[35] Adopted in April 2008, FCC rules dictate the technical standards and protocols governing CMAS and require alerts to be (1) sent to areas no larger than the county level and (2) limited to 90 characters.[36] Several state

---

[34]FCC re-chartered the Communications Security, Reliability and Interoperability Council, which is comprised of representatives from federal, state, tribal and local governments, various sectors of the communications industry, and non-profit organizations. *Public Notice,* DA 13-173 (Feb. 12, 2013), 2013 Westlaw 519, 447. The Council advises FCC on actions the Commission can take to promote the security, reliability, and interoperability of communications systems. At the time of our report, FCC had not published what items the Council would be reviewing.

[35]CMAS enables government officials to target emergency alerts to specific geographic areas through cell towers (e.g., lower Manhattan), which pushes the information to dedicated receivers in CMAS-enabled mobile devices.

[36]47 C.F.R. §§ 10.430 and 10.450. FCC rules do not preclude participating wireless carriers from targeting geographic areas more granular than at the county level.

and local alerting authorities we spoke with raised concerns about the possibility of over alerting the public with mobile alerts since the alerts may not geo-target the specific area affected. The 90-character message limitations of these alerts were also raised as a challenge by FEMA and other alerting authorities to sending out clear and accurate alerts, as alerts may not contain enough information to be useful. For example, according to officials in one state, the National Weather Service issued a flash flood warning via CMAS that was distributed throughout a large county, which is roughly the size of the state of Connecticut, when only one small area of the county was affected. According to state officials, some citizens were confused when they received this alert as they were not located in the affected area, and there was very little information contained in the 90-character alert to clarify the specific area affected. In addition, an evacuation notice accompanied the flash flood warning, and the local emergency management authority was unprepared when citizens called them for additional information.[37] Officials stated that some citizens might ignore or opt out of future mobile alerts if they received previous alerts that were not applicable to them. The Commercial Mobile Service Alert Advisory Committee,[38] which recommended technical standards and protocols for CMAS in 2007,[39] recommended reviewing and updating its recommendations periodically based on advances in technology and experiences in deployment, especially related to geo-targeting.[40] As previously mentioned, FCC plans to have a federal advisory committee review the CMAS rules, including those related to geo-targeting and character limits. Technological advancements and experiences in using the system since 2008 may warrant a review on a more specific level of geo-targeting and expanded character limits

---

[37]According to FEMA, some specific phone models improperly displayed an evacuation notice with the flash-flood warning because of phone-programming error. FEMA said it does not edit or restrict the content or targeting of messages sent through IPAWS, as long as the target zone is within the bounds of the public-alerting authorities' jurisdiction, as indicated when applying for IPAWS authentication.

[38]The committee was chaired by the FCC chairman and included 42 other members, representing stakeholders in all levels of government and the private sector.

[39]*In the Matter of the Commercial Mobile Alert System,* 22 FCC Rcd. 21,975 (2007).

[40]FCC officials noted that both the geo-targeting and message length rules were a consensus-based product of a government and industry advisory committee in which FEMA and NOAA participated and that the rules were adopted pursuant to a notice and opportunity for comment rulemaking.

for mobile alerts than was previously possible. Such changes to CMAS could make state and local authorities more likely to use these alerts and the public less likely to opt out of the service.

- **Insufficient public outreach.** According to federal, state, and local officials we contacted, the public is generally unaware of IPAWS capabilities, especially alerts sent to mobile phones. Although FEMA officials told us that a training course to educate the public is under development, FEMA has conducted limited outreach to date to inform the general public about IPAWS alerts and capabilities beyond information on the FEMA website. Executive Order No. 13407 directs DHS to provide public education on using, accessing, and responding to the public alert and warning system. Because of limited public outreach, some state and local alerting authorities expressed concern that the public may ignore or opt out of receiving IPAWS alerts, even though these alerts may provide important, life-saving information. While FEMA has made efforts to improve outreach efforts with IPAWS stakeholders since 2009, FEMA officials said they have limited resources and experience in educating the general public on IPAWS. In previous work, we identified key practices for planning a consumer education campaign, including (1) defining goals and objectives; (2) analyzing the situation; (3) identifying stakeholders; (4) identifying resources; (5) researching target audiences; (6) developing consistent, clear messages; (7) identifying credible messenger(s); (8) designing media mix; and (9) establishing metrics to measure success.[41] Public outreach that includes these key practices could help ensure that the public is better informed about IPAWS capabilities.

- **Limited resources to implement IPAWS.** While there is no charge to send messages through IPAWS, there are underlying costs to purchasing the software and equipment needed to integrate with IPAWS, costs that state and local public alerting authorities said can act as a barrier to implementation in difficult financial times.[42] According to the FEMA survey of public alerting authorities,

---

[41]GAO, *Digital Television Transition: Increased Federal Planning and Risk Management Could Further Facilitate the DTV Transition,* GAO-08-43 (Washington, D.C.: Nov. 19, 2007).

[42]According to FEMA, funding from the Homeland Security Grant Program and the Tr bal Homeland Security Grant Program may be used to enhance existing or establish new alert and warning programs.

decreased revenues and a lack of grant funding at all levels of government were reported as primary reasons for authorities' inability to purchase and sustain alerting systems.[43] In addition, the FEMA survey found that while most state-level alerting authorities reported having full-time staff, many local authorities might only have part-time or volunteer staff and very limited budgets.

In addition to these barriers, there are some long-standing weaknesses that continue to limit the effectiveness of the national-level EAS since we last reported on this topic in 2009, including a lack of redundancy in how national-level EAS messages are disseminated to the public.[44] FEMA is making progress in increasing redundancy between the FEMA operations center and designated PEP stations through its deployment of a PEP satellite network. However, FEMA continues to rely solely on radio and television broadcast for a national-level EAS alert because the national-level EAS is not currently integrated with IPAWS capabilities. As a result, FEMA lacks alternative means of reaching EAS participants should a point in the daisy chain distribution system fail. Moreover, large portions of the population would likely not be reached by a national-level alert—specifically all those who are not watching television or listening to the radio at the time of the alert. Executive Order No. 13407 directs DHS to ensure presidential alerting capabilities under all conditions and enable delivery of coordinated messages to the American people through as many communication pathways as practicable. In addition, while Executive Order No. 13407 specifies that the public-alerting system should provide warnings to non-English speakers and individuals with disabilities, it remains difficult for a national-level alert to reach these distinct segments of the population. While the President has never initiated a national-level alert, according to FEMA, such an alert would be provided in English and only through radio and television broadcasts, which may not be accessible to individuals with disabilities.[45] For example, according to the National Council on Disability, most disaster warnings broadcast via radio and television may not be accessible to

---

[43]FEMA, *IPAWS Inventory & Evaluation Assessment Report*, December 2011.

[44]In 2007 and 2009, we reported that a lack of alternative means, or lack of redundancy, in reaching EAS participants should its primary connection fail, makes the EAS daisy chain prone to failure. See GAO-07-411 and GAO-09-834.

[45]FCC officials noted that nothing in FCC's rules precludes transmission of non-English alerts. Alerts sent via IPAWS are provided in any language the alerting authorities can use when developing a CAP-formatted alert message.

people with hearing or vision disabilities.[46] IPAWS, which can transmit CAP-formatted messages to specialized alerting devices for individuals with disabilities and in non-English languages, could help address some of these limitations if it were integrated with the national-level EAS.

Most Reporting EAS Participants Received and Retransmitted the Test Alert, but Federal Efforts to Address Identified Weaknesses Are Limited

Results of the Nationwide EAS Test

Our analysis of FCC data found that approximately 82 percent of reporting broadcasters (radio and television) and cable operators received the November 2011 nationwide test alert.[47] Although FEMA has been working to implement IPAWS, the November 2011 nationwide EAS test used the traditional national-level alert system (i.e., EAS daisy-chain relay distribution system) and did not include new IPAWS capabilities.[48] Broadcasters' and cable operators' reception of the test alert varied widely by state. As shown in figure 3, the reception of the alert ranged from approximately 6 percent (in Oregon) to 100 percent (in Delaware) among the states. FCC, FEMA, broadcasters, and state alerting authorities in Oregon attributed the low reception rate to the absence of a

---

[46]National Council on Disability, *Effective Emergency Management: Making Improvements for Communities and People with Disabilities* (Aug. 12, 2009).

[47]FCC required that EAS participants report to FCC on whether they received the test alert, but many did not do so. As of January 2013, we found that about 61 percent of broadcasters and cable operators had submitted the report as required. Our analysis is based on broadcasters and cable operators that submitted information to FCC that we determined usable for our reporting purposes.

[48]As previously mentioned, these systems are not integrated, and FEMA is in discussions with the White House to determine the use of IPAWS during a presidential alert.

PEP station in the state at the time of the test.[49] Without a PEP station, broadcasters and cable operators in Oregon were directed to monitor a Portland-based public radio station, which reported receiving poor audio quality of the alert from its designated monitoring source—the National Public Radio satellite network.

Figure 3: Percentage of Broadcasters and Cable Operators by State That Received the Nationwide EAS Test Alert

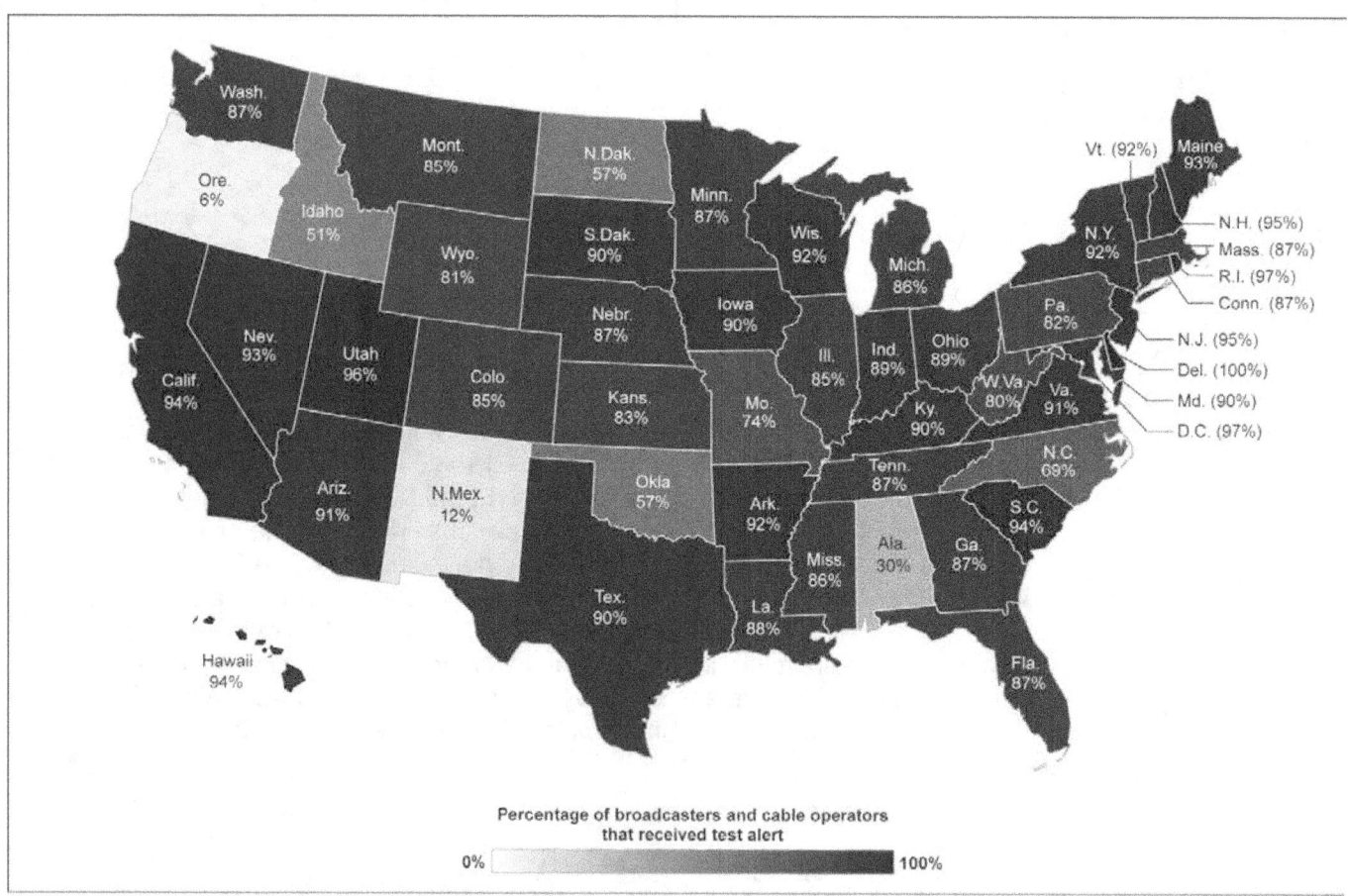

Percentage of broadcasters and cable operators that received test alert

0%   100%

Source: GAO Analysis of FCC data.

Note: This figure represents broadcasters' and cable operators' reception rates by state and does not include reception rates from U.S. territories. Additionally, FCC excused Alaska from the nationwide EAS test because of severe weather at the time of the test.

[49]Since that time, as part of FEMA's PEP Station Expansion and Modernization Program, a PEP station in Oregon became operational in December 2012.

Once EAS participants received the national-level test alert, they were required to retransmit the audio signal to other EAS participants, as designated in state EAS plans, for the daisy chain distribution system to work. Our analysis of FCC data found that 61 percent of reporting broadcasters and cable operators were able to retransmit the alert to stations that were designated to monitor the retransmitting station. The retransmission rate of the test alert by broadcasters and cable operators also varied widely among the states ranging from approximately 4 percent (in Oregon) to 88 percent (in New Jersey). FCC does not know the potential percentage of the American people who did not receive the alert because, officials noted, the nationwide EAS test was designed to assess EAS performance rather than to determine the percentage of public receipt of the test. Therefore, it is unknown what percentage of the American people failed to receive the test.

Key reasons for EAS participants' failure to receive and retransmit the national-level test alert included (1) PEP station reception failure, (2) poor audio quality, (3) shortened test length, (4) outdated monitoring assignments, and (5) equipment failure.

- **PEP station reception failure.** FEMA reported that 3 of the 63 PEP stations were unable to receive and retransmit the alert due to technical reasons. These PEP stations were located in New Mexico, Alabama, and American Samoa. Failures at those stations significantly contributed to low national-level alert reception rates in those states and that territory. In particular, our analysis of FCC data found that nearly 90 percent of broadcasters in New Mexico, almost 70 percent of broadcasters in Alabama, and 100 percent of broadcasters in American Samoa failed to receive the national-level alert. According to FEMA, connectivity issues with the specialized EAS equipment used at the PEP stations were the reasons for the failure. As previously mentioned, FEMA plans to modernize PEP stations with a dedicated satellite network, and officials expect this dedicated network to provide more reliable connection to the PEP stations when fully operational by fall 2013.

- **Poor audio quality.** FCC also reported that poor audio quality of the national-level alert signal resulted in problems ranging from some broadcasters' receiving a garbled and degraded audio message to others' receiving a duplicate alert tone that caused equipment to malfunction. These audio problems resulted in some stations' being unable to retransmit the test alert. According to FEMA, the reported poor audio quality was due, in part, to a feedback loop that occurred when equipment at a single PEP station rebroadcasted the original message back to FEMA. This audio message was then transmitted by FEMA over the original audio message, degrading the audio. Therefore, fewer stations were able to receive, and thus retransmit, the alert to their designated station(s). EAS participants we met with consistently stated that the poor audio quality during the nationwide EAS test was a significant problem. For example, state and local alerting authorities, broadcaster associations, and individual broadcast stations we contacted stated that connectivity and audio problems occurred during the nationwide test. Officials from one state broadcasters association said that broadcasters in their state only received 10 seconds of the national-level alert signal with only five or six words of the message and then 20 seconds of dead air for the remainder of the test. They also stated that problems with the audio resulted in the alerts not being retransmitted to other stations in their state.

- **Shortened test length.** The nationwide EAS test was originally scheduled to last 3 minutes, but was shortened to 30 seconds. According to an industry trade association, the announcement to change the test length came about 2 weeks prior to the test. Because of the shortened test length, some broadcasters and cable operators were unable to receive or retransmit the national-level alert. According to FEMA, the test was shortened to mitigate concerns from the cable industry that the public who could not hear the audio portion of the test would be unable to tell if the alert was a test or a real alert solely from the television screen display. More specifically, FCC instructed broadcasters to use an on-screen slide just before the test to announce that the following message would be a test and not an actual alert. However, according to officials from an industry trade association, some EAS participants, namely some cable operators, were unable to provide this background screen during the nationwide test. In these cases, since FCC chose to use a live alert code to resemble an actual nationwide test, there was no visual cue that a test was taking place. There was concern that this could adversely affect some segments of the public, especially individuals who were unable to hear the audio portion indicating a test was taking place. According to representatives from industry trade associations, use of a test code for future nationwide EAS tests could help ensure that all segments of the population understand that a nationwide test, rather than an actual national emergency, is taking place.

- **Outdated monitoring assignments.** FCC noted that some state EAS plans that designate the monitoring assignments are outdated and its review of the EAS test results revealed some confusion among some EAS participants of monitoring assignments. We found that as of February 2013, out of 33 state and District of Columbia EAS plans available on FCC's website, 16 state plans were dated 2009 or earlier, with 3 of these plans dated in the 1990s. Additionally, 18 state plans were not available on FCC's website with the link to one website leading to information completely unrelated to the state.[50] FEMA reported that if monitoring assignments in the state EAS plans are not followed or the state EAS plans are not up-to-date, EAS participants may not receive and relay the messages. According to FEMA, several EAS participants reported not being able to receive the national-level alert from their assigned sources, and as a result, they were unable to relay the alert.

- **Equipment failures.** Because of specific equipment failures, some broadcasters could not receive or retransmit the national-level alert. FCC reported that approximately 5 percent of EAS participants responding to its data collection effort reported that hardware, equipment, or configuration problems precluded them from receiving the national-level alert.

Limited Federal Efforts to Address Identified Issues

At the time of our review, FCC and FEMA had taken limited steps to address problems identified in the nationwide EAS test. According to FEMA officials, the poor audio quality that was experienced during the test is being addressed, in part, with the deployment of a dedicated PEP satellite network, but the remaining issues have yet to be resolved. FEMA officials told us that it will take a combination of FCC rulemaking, developing best practices, and correcting technical issues to address the problems that were identified during the nationwide test, but implementing some of these actions could likely take years. According to FCC officials, a working group, in coordination with FEMA, has been examining these issues, but neither agency could identify progress made by the group more than a year after the test. In commenting on a draft of this report, FCC told us it issued its final report on the results of the nationwide EAS test on April 12, 2013.[51] According to FCC officials, one of the reasons for

---

[50]According to FCC, some state emergency communication committees maintain their state plans as official use only documents and do not post them on the Internet.

[51]FCC, *Strengthening the Emergency Alert System (EAS): Lessons Learned from the Nationwide EAS Test*, April 2013. The report can be found at http://hraunfoss.fcc.gov/edocs_public/attachmatch//DOC-320152A1.pdf.

the delay in issuing a final report on the test result was their effort to collect more data from EAS participants. FCC continued to accept paper reports on the test results from EAS participants for about a year after the test was conducted, despite the December 27, 2011 deadline for electronically submitting the test results. EAS participants and state and local alerting authorities we contacted said that they were not aware of FCC taking any actions to address identified issues, and as a result, their ability to make improvements and prepare for future tests is limited. Concerning future tests, FCC rules require a nationwide EAS test to be conducted periodically,[52] but it is uncertain when the next test will occur. FEMA officials told us that they are continuing to work with FCC in determining corrective actions from the test results and will not hold another test until corrective actions are complete. As we have previously reported, regular nationwide EAS testing is essential to ensure that the system will work as intended during an emergency.[53]

FCC recognizes that outdated state EAS plans contributed to some of the reception and retransmission problems during the EAS test, and is being more proactive in requesting states to submit updated plans. FCC officials stated that updating state EAS plans would be valuable to ensure that the monitoring assignments for the broadcast stations remain accurate when a national-level alert is activated. However, as of October 2012, FCC has received 7 of 50 updated state EAS plans.[54] Officials stated that they would continue to ask state emergency communications committees to submit updated EAS plans to review, but that FCC has no authority to require the filing of EAS plans. As a result, FCC is unable to fully verify that states are keeping EAS monitoring assignments up to date. In addition, some EAS participants we spoke with are waiting for more guidance from FCC, including anticipated changes in rules governing EAS. For example, FCC officials told us that they plan to issue a notice of proposed rulemaking sometime in 2013 seeking comment on issues identified from the nationwide EAS test.

---

[52]*In the Matter of Review of the Emergency Alert System*, 26 FCC Rcd. 1,460, 1,479 (2011). According to FCC rules, EAS testing is to be conducted no more frequently than annually.

[53]GAO-09-834.

[54]An EAS plan is also prepared for the District of Columbia and some territories.

EAS participants and state and local alerting authorities we spoke with stated that there are several actions that FCC, in conjunction with FEMA, could take that would assist EAS participants in preparing, conducting, and reporting on future nationwide EAS test alerts. These actions include (1) issuing an after-action plan to help identify and address problems that occurred during the test, (2) conducting regular and frequent testing of EAS to ensure the system works as intended, and (3) providing guidance to update state EAS plans to incorporate IPAWS (e.g., guidance could be EAS plan templates, best practices, good examples).

Conclusions

FEMA has made progress since 2009 in developing a more comprehensive, integrated nationwide public-alerting system. FEMA has improved the capabilities of IPAWS by bringing the IPAWS alert aggregator online and integrating it with multiple alerting systems, including HazCollect and CMAS. However, for IPAWS to become fully operational, several areas of concern need to be addressed. In particular, additional guidance for state and local alerting authorities on specific steps to integrate and test their public-alerting systems with IPAWS components would help to provide assurance on the interoperability and effectiveness of IPAWS and facilitate its implementation. Furthermore, according to public-alerting authorities we contacted, without additional guidance on IPAWS implementation and consideration of CMAS rules, state and local alerting authorities we contacted were reluctant to fully integrate their systems with IPAWS and rely on IPAWS as a comprehensive public-alerting system. In addition, a concerted effort to educate state and local governments, the private sector, and the American people on the functions of the public-alerting system is necessary to inform them on how to access, use, and respond to emergency alert messages. Using key practices for conducting a public education campaign—such as defining goals and objectives, identifying stakeholders and resources, and developing clear and consistent messages—could enable FEMA, which has limited experience educating the general public on IPAWS, to more effectively and efficiently inform the American people on how to access and respond to potentially life-saving emergency alerts.

FEMA has also expanded the number of PEP stations and enhanced satellite connectivity to improve direct coverage and dependability of the national-level EAS. However, as long as the national-level EAS remains independent from IPAWS, portions of the population, including individuals with disabilities and non-English speakers, will be less likely to receive or fully understand presidential alerts disseminated only through the EAS daisy chain. If integrated, CMAS, in particular, is capable of providing alerts in different formats, including emitting unique ring tone and vibration cadences for those who have hearing or visual impairments, which would increase the likelihood that individuals with disabilities could be informed that a national-level alert is being issued. Furthermore, integrating EAS into IPAWS would provide system redundancy for national-level alerts.

FEMA and FCC held the first-ever test of the national-level EAS in November 2011, an important step. However, the results of the nationwide EAS test—which a number of EAS participants could not effectively receive or retransmit—show that the reliability of the traditional EAS system remains questionable. At the time of our review, we found that FEMA and FCC had taken limited steps to address problems identified by EAS participants. In addition, some state EAS plans and monitoring assignments are outdated, in part, because state emergency communications committees are waiting for more guidance from FCC, including changes in rules governing EAS. Although states are not required to update and submit state EAS plans, FCC could help facilitate the process by providing additional guidance. Finally, while FCC rules call for periodic nationwide EAS testing, FCC and FEMA currently have not scheduled another nationwide test. Without ongoing, regular nationwide testing of the relay distribution system, there is no assurance the EAS would work should the President need to activate it to communicate with the American people.

Recommendations for Executive Action

To ensure that IPAWS is fully functional and capable of distributing alerts through multiple pathways as intended, we recommend that the Secretary of Homeland Security direct the Administrator of FEMA to take the following four actions:

- In conjunction with FCC, establish guidance (e.g., procedures, best practices) that will assist participating state and local alerting authorities to fully implement and test IPAWS components and ensure integration and interoperability.

- In conjunction with FCC and NOAA, conduct coordinated outreach to educate the American public on IPAWS capabilities, especially CMAS.

- Develop a plan to disseminate a national-level alert via IPAWS to increase redundancy and communicate presidential alerts through multiple pathways.

- In conjunction with FCC, develop and implement a strategy for regularly testing the national-level EAS, including examining the need for a national test code, developing milestones and time frames, improving data collection efforts, and reporting on after-action plans.

To ensure that CMAS is effectively used and that the EAS relay distribution network is capable of reliably communicating national-level alerts, we recommend that the Chairman of FCC, in conjunction with FEMA, take the following two actions:

- Review and update rules governing CMAS, including those related to geo-targeting, character limitations, and testing procedures.

- Provide states with additional guidance (e.g., templates of EAS plan) to facilitate completion of updated state EAS plans that include IPAWS-compatible equipment.

Agency Comments

We provided a draft of this report to DHS, FCC, and the Department of Commerce for their review and comment. In response, DHS concurred with all of the report's recommendations to improve IPAWS capabilities. In its written comments, DHS provided examples of actions FEMA will undertake to address the recommendations. For example, DHS noted that FEMA intends to create toolkits for state and local alerting authorities that will include alerting and governance best practices, technology requirements, and operation and usage information on IPAWS. Regarding efforts to improve nationwide EAS testing, DHS indicated that FEMA plans to work with federal partners, including FCC, to create a national test code, develop milestones and timeframes for future testing, improve data collection efforts, and report on after-action plans. See appendix III for written comments from DHS.

In commenting on the draft report, FCC did not state whether it agreed or disagreed with the report's recommendations. FCC noted that it issued a final report on the results of the nationwide EAS test on April 12, 2013, and we believe the report includes potential actions that could address our recommendations in the future. For example, the April 2013 report includes recommendations for FCC to commence a rulemaking proceeding on state EAS plans and to encourage the groups that typically develop state EAS plans to ensure that the plans contain accurate EAS monitoring assignments. Other recommendations in FCC's April 2013 report include commencing a rulemaking proceeding to examine equipment-performance issues during activation of a test, and developing a new Nationwide EAS Test Reporting System database to improve filing electronic data from EAS participants. FCC stated that it will conduct a review of CMAS rules, as we recommended in this report, and also noted that it will work with FEMA to develop a strategy for regular testing of EAS. See appendix IV for written comments from FCC.

The Department of Commerce provided technical comments from its component agency NOAA, and we incorporated them as appropriated. In the comments, NOAA stated that it believes our report does an accurate job in assessing the nationwide EAS test results and the current state of IPAWS. With respect to our recommendation on conducting outreach, NOAA believes the outreach should be conducted in conjunction with FCC and NOAA, and we made the suggested revision.

In addition to written comments, DHS and FCC provided technical comments on the draft report, which we incorporated as appropriate.

As agreed upon with your office, unless you publicly announce the contents of this report earlier, we plan no further distribution until 30 days from the report date. At that time, we will send copies of this report to appropriate congressional committees, the Secretary of Homeland Security, and the Chairman of FCC. In addition, the report is available at no charge on our website at http://www.gao.gov.

If you or your staff have any questions concerning this report, please contact me at (202) 512-2834 or goldsteinm@gao.gov. Contact points for our Offices of Congressional Relations and Public Affairs may be found on the last page of this report. Key contributors to this report are listed in appendix V.

Mark Goldstein
Director, Physical Infrastructure Issues

Appendix I: Objectives, Scope, and Methodology

This report provides information on federal efforts to integrate various public-alerting systems and modernize the Emergency Alert System (EAS). Specifically, the report examines (1) how the capabilities of the Integrated Public Alert and Warning System (IPAWS) have changed since 2009 and what barriers, if any, are affecting its implementation and (2) the results of the nationwide EAS test and federal efforts under way to address identified weaknesses.

To obtain information on both objectives of this report, we interviewed officials from the Federal Emergency Management Agency (FEMA), Federal Communications Commission (FCC), Department of Homeland Security, and National Oceanic and Atmospheric Administration (NOAA). We spoke with representatives from national trade industry groups, including the National Emergency Management Association, National Association of Broadcasters, National Cable and Telecommunications Association, CTIA-The Wireless Association, and National Alliance of State Broadcasters Associations, to obtain stakeholders' perspective on the results of the first nationwide EAS test and federal efforts to implement IPAWS. We also spoke with representatives from the satellite industry (DIRECTV), an EAS equipment manufacturer (Monroe Electronics), and the National Council on Disability to gather their views on IPAWS implementation and the nationwide EAS test. We conducted interviews with selected state and local alerting authorities, state emergency-communication-committee chairs, state broadcasting associations, and selected local broadcasters. We nonstatistically selected a sample of six locations—California, Kentucky, Oklahoma, Oregon, Wisconsin, and the District of Columbia—to obtain information from state and local officials on any barriers to implementing IPAWS and potential remedies for addressing any identified barriers, as well as to determine any problems associated with the nationwide EAS test. We selected these states and locality because some had (1) other public-alerting systems, in addition to the EAS; (2) alerting systems that are capable of providing alerts for individuals with disabilities and limited English; and (3) experienced a breakdown of test alert dissemination during the nationwide EAS test. We also selected these states and localities because some had been authenticated to be an IPAWS-alerting authority and they were geographically diverse. To obtain a regional perspective on implementing IPAWS and testing the EAS, we also spoke with officials from FEMA regional offices. Because we conducted targeted interviews, our results are not generalizable to all states and localities. Table 1 provides more detailed information on the state and localities we selected and the entities we interviewed.

Table 2: State and Local Interviews

State/Locality	Public alerting authorities	State association of broadcasters and local broadcasters	FEMA regional office
California	• California Emergency Management Agency • Office of Emergency Services, Humboldt County Sherriff's Office • County of San Diego Office of Emergency Services	California Broadcasters Association	Region IX
District of Columbia	District of Columbia Homeland Security and Emergency Management Agency	WTOP-FM	Region III
Kentucky	• Kentucky Division of Emergency Management • Daviess County Emergency Management Office	Kentucky Broadcasters Association	Region IV
Oklahoma	• Oklahoma Department of Emergency Management	• Oklahoma Association of Broadcasters • KTUL-FM • Clear Channel Radio in Oklahoma City	Region VI
Oregon	• Oregon Office of Emergency Management • Portland Bureau of Emergency Management	Oregon Association of Broadcasters	Region X
Wisconsin	• Wisconsin Emergency Management	• Wisconsin Broadcasters Association • WISC-TV • Wisconsin Educational Communications Board	Region V[a]

Source: GAO.

[a]We were unable to interview FEMA officials in Region V, despite our attempt to contact them.

To obtain information on how the capabilities of IPAWS have changed since 2009 and what barriers, if any, affect its implementation, we also reviewed and analyzed agency documents and literature since 2009. We reviewed documents on IPAWS program planning, including the 2010 IPAWS program management plan, and assessed actions that have been taken to determine if systems and standards are operational. We also attended a number of IPAWS webinars to obtain training and information that are provided to public-alerting authorities. We reviewed FEMA's *IPAWS Inventory and Evaluation Assessment Report*, which surveyed 3,314 state, territorial, tribal, and local emergency management agencies to analyze gaps between existing public-alerting capabilities and IPAWS and includes recommendations for IPAWS integration. The survey was conducted mostly by telephone with structured questionnaires over a 2-year period from January 2010 through December 2011 and specific

procedures were followed to identify emergency management personnel
for the sites at each level. We assessed the survey's methodology and
determined that the estimates from it that we cite are sufficiently valid for
use in our report. Specifically, we assessed the survey methodology
against the Office of Management and Budget's *Standards and
Guidelines for Statistical Surveys*. We did not otherwise verify, however,
the findings and conclusions from the report.

To obtain information on the results of the nationwide EAS test and
federal efforts to address any identified weaknesses, we reviewed and
analyzed agency data and documents. Specifically, we examined FCC's
and FEMA's preliminary reports on the nationwide EAS test results; FCC
orders and rules on EAS; FCC's website on the nationwide EAS test;
FEMA's EAS Best Practices Guide; and briefing documents from FEMA
and NOAA. We analyzed FCC's data from EAS participants to determine
the percentage of radio and television broadcasters and cable operators
that received and retransmitted the national-level alert on a statewide
basis. We analyzed FCC's data for 49 states; we did not include Alaska
since it was excused from the nationwide test because of severe weather
conditions. To determine the reliability of the data used in this report, we
reviewed relevant documentation and interviewed agency officials about
their processes for reviewing the data and ensuring their accuracy. We
also ensured that FCC data were sufficiently reliable for our review. We
reviewed and analyzed state EAS plans that were posted on FCC's
website to determine if the state's EAS plans were current. We
interviewed FCC officials to confirm that the information on FCC's website
is current.

We conducted this performance audit from June 2012 through April 2013,
in accordance with generally accepted government auditing standards.
Those standards require that we plan and perform the audit to obtain
sufficient, appropriate evidence to provide a reasonable basis for our
findings and conclusions based on our audit objectives. We believe that
the evidence obtained provides a reasonable basis for our findings and
conclusions based on our audit objectives.

Appendix II: FEMA's Progress Addressing Responsibilities of the Secretary of Homeland Security under Executive Order No. 13407

Responsibilities	Status/progress/timeline
Inventory and assess existing alert infrastructure	Issued the *IPAWS Inventory and Evaluation Assessment Report* in January 2012. This report surveyed and assessed public-alerting authorities in the United States between 2009 and 2011.
Develop alert standards and Protocols	Formally adopted the Commercial Mobile Alerting System (CMAS) Specification in December 2009.
	Formally adopted the Common Alerting Protocol (CAP) standard for IPAWS in September 2010.
Geo-targeted, risk-based alerts[a]	Implemented CMAS. Wireless carriers began issuing geo-targeted CMAS alerts in April 2012; NOAA started sending geo-targeted CMAS messages in June 2012.
Alerts for non-English speakers and the disabled	Hosted biannual roundtables for industry experts, federal agencies, and advocacy organizations representing Americans with access and functional needs to discuss emergency alerting.
	Shared lessons learned and best practices for communicating to Americans with access and functional needs through the EAS to FCC. For example, encouraged FCC to consider EAS rule changes or clarifications for broadcasters with regard to: (1) display size, color, background contrast, and speed of text crawl during EAS alert and (2) use of a test code for future nationwide testing of EAS.
Augment infrastructure	Expanded the number of primary entry point (PEP) stations to 65 total—31 PEP stations were either modernized or built since 2009. Anticipates a total of 77 PEP stations by fall 2013 directly covering 90 percent of the American people. Added satellite connectivity in 50 PEP stations.
	Integrated NOAA alerting systems to allow public-alerting authorities to send non-weather emergency messages through HazCollect; allowed NOAA to send mobile alerts beginning 2012.
Conduct training and testing	Released IPAWS online training for public-alerting authorities in December 2011. Hosts monthly webinars for developers and alerting practitioners.
	Conducted two statewide EAS tests in Alaska in January 2010 and 2011; conducted the first nationwide EAS test on November 9, 2011.
	Conducted CMAS test in New York City in December 2011. Conducts a required monthly test of CMAS on the third Wednesday of each month.
Provide public education on uses and access to the public alert and warning system	Maintains a public website on IPAWS.
Consult, coordinate, and cooperate with private sector	Hosts monthly webinars for developers and alerting practitioners.
	Participated in federal working groups and roundtables.
	Participates in industry conferences, demonstrations, and panels.
Administer EAS as component of public alert and warning system	Acts as executive agent for EAS, maintaining the PEP stations.
Ensure presidential alert and warning capability under all conditions	Maintains EAS and PEP stations.
	Deploying a dedicated PEP satellite network.

Source: GAO analysis of Exec. Order No. 13407 and FEMA.

[a]Ensure the capability to distr bute alerts on the basis of geographic location, risks, or personal user preferences.

Appendix III: Comments from the Department of Homeland Security

U.S. Department of Homeland Security
Washington, DC 20528

April 12, 2013

Mark Goldstein
Director, Physical Infrastructure Issues
U.S. Government Accountability Office
441 G Street, NW
Washington, DC 20548

Re: Draft Report GAO-13-375, "EMERGENCY ALERTING: Capabilities Have Improved but
    Additional Guidance and Testing Are Needed"

Dear Mr. Goldstein:

Thank you for the opportunity to review and comment on this draft report. The U.S. Department
of Homeland Security (DHS) appreciates the U.S. Government Accountability Office's (GAO's)
work in planning and conducting its review and issuing this report.

The Department is pleased to note GAO's recognition of progress made by the Federal
Emergency Management Agency (FEMA) to improve National Continuity Programs Integrated
Public Alert and Warning System (IPAWS) capabilities over the past three and a half years. We
appreciate that GAO recognizes our initiatives to refine and enhance an effective, reliable,
integrated, flexible, and comprehensive system to alert and warn the American people.

The draft report contained four recommendations, with which the Department concurs.
Specifically, GAO recommended that the Secretary of Homeland Security direct the FEMA
Administrator:

Recommendation 1: In conjunction with the FCC, establish guidance (e.g., procedures, best
practices) that will assist participating state and local alerting authorities to fully implement and
test IPAWS components and ensure integration and interoperability.

Response: Concur. FEMA recognizes the Federal Communications Commission's (FCC's)
rule-making role and will continue to work with the FCC and other federal partners to assist state
and local alerting authorities to implement and test IPAWS. FEMA will leverage existing
resources and create toolkits for alerting authorities. These toolkits will address alerting and
governance best practices, technology requirements, and IPAWS operation and usage, as well as
testing, exercises, and training. The toolkits will contain instructions describing qualification of
an authorized IPAWS alerting authority, advice on how to build and strengthen relationships
with the private sector and other alerting partners, and information resources to help educate the
public about alerts and warnings. FEMA strives to work with all stakeholders, including the
FCC, to ensure IPAWS integration and interoperability.

Estimated Completion Date: To Be Determined.

Recommendation 2: Conduct outreach to educate the American public on IPAWS capabilities, especially CMAS.

Response: Concur. FEMA will collaborate closely with federal, state, local, non-profit and advocacy organizations, the private sector, and the media to accelerate our efforts to ensure the American public understands how IPAWS functions and how to respond to alerts and warnings from public safety officials. Since Wireless Emergency Alerts (WEAs) sent through the IPAWS Commercial Mobile Alerting System (CMAS) interface are of particular interest to the American public, our educational campaigns will focus primarily on WEAs.

To date, in addition to conducting substantial educational outreach to the public, FEMA has:

- Distributed a State Toolkit for Alerting Authorities around the country that contains coordinates messaging on WEAs, talking points for background on WEAs and local media interviews, templates for a state press release, a blog, WEA Fact Sheet, and FAQ document
- Created a brief on-line course for the public, titled "IPAWS and the American People"
- Wrote a series of informational fact sheets about IPAWS initiatives, programs, and systems, tailored for several specific audiences
- Participated in strategically selected conferences and events, providing presentations, workshops, and end-to-end technical demonstrations about IPAWS
- Developed and updated relevant information on the IPAWS Website
- Developed and released a 5-minute comprehensive IPAWS overview video and linked it to the IPAWS Website homepage
- Arranged national, regional, and local media interviews for radio, wire services, TV and newspapers on WEAs, including the Weather Channel, Associated Press, The New York Times, Congressional Quarterly, NBC-5 television in Dallas, Texas, Federal News Radio, WTOP radio in Washington, DC, various dot.com sites, and specialty press such as Emergency Management Magazine
- Issued (Twitter) tweets and several press releases about possible WEAs during recent severe weather events. These tweets and press releases included links to the WEA FAQs on READY.gov
- Posted a video on the FEMA Assistant Administrator for FEMA's National Continuity Programs Website educating the public about WEAs and how to prepare for hurricanes

In the future, in addition to continuing current initiatives, FEMA plans to:
- Create a comprehensive toolkit to address alerting and governance best practices, technology requirements, IPAWS operation and usage, and testing, training, and exercises. The toolkit will offer assistance and instructions on how to qualify to be an authorized IPAWS alerting authority, advice on how to build and strengthen relationships with private-sector and other alerting partners, and resources for educating the public about alerts and warnings.
- Work with federal partners (e.g., FCC, NOAA, DOJ) and the Ad Council to create and disseminate Public Service Announcements nationwide

2

- Work with state partners to develop education campaigns in their states that incorporate their own resources, as well as IPAWS and Ready.gov
- Engage the media and provide the information they need to produce accurate, interesting, and positive IPAWS and WEA news coverage

Estimated Completion Date: To Be Determined.

Recommendation 3: Develop a plan to disseminate a national-level alert via IPAWS to increase redundancy and communicate presidential alerts through multiple pathways.

Response: Concur. The national-level EAS was established in 1995 to provide a reliable pathway for the President to communicate with the American public in extreme situations. The national-level EAS is a contingency program for the President when other forms of communications are not reliable or available. FEMA administers and manages the PEP program to support national-level EAS capabilities through hardened, resilient radio stations. Current operations allow a national-level alert to be initiated via IPAWS over multiple pathways directing citizens to the "National EAS" as a robust, resilient capability to survive all hazards. Distributing the Presidential message over multiple pathways will require coordinating and identifying additional operational requirements with The White House.

Estimated Completion Date: To Be Determined.

Recommendation 4: In conjunction with FCC, develop and implement a strategy for regularly testing the national-level EAS, including examining the need for a national test code, developing milestones and timeframes, improving data collection efforts, and reporting on after-action plans.

Response: Concur. FEMA looks forward to continued collaboration with the FCC using the 2011 national-level EAS test plan as a foundation to develop and implement a strategy for regular future national-level EAS testing. FEMA will also work with federal partners, including the Executive Office of the President and the FCC, to create a national test code, develop milestones and timeframes, improve data collection efforts, and report on after-action plans.

Estimated Completion Date: To Be Determined.

Again, thank you for the opportunity to review and comment on this draft report. Technical comments were previously provided under separate cover. Please feel free to contact me if you have any questions. We look forward to working with you in the future.

Sincerely,

Jim H. Crumpacker
Director
Departmental GAO-OIG Liaison Office

3

Appendix IV: Comments from the Federal Communications Commission

Federal Communications Commission
Washington, D.C. 20554

April 12, 2013

Mark Goldstein
Director
Physical Infrastructure Issues
Government Accountability Office
441 G Street, NW
Washington, DC 20548

Dear Mr. Goldstein:

Thank you for the opportunity to review GAO's draft report on Emergency Alerting. The Federal Communications Commission's (FCC) specific comments to various parts of the draft report are in the attached table.

We would like to update you on a few matters that are discussed in the draft report. First, the draft GAO report notes that the FCC has not issued an "official" report on the results of the November 9, 2011 Nationwide EAS Test. On April 12, 2013, the FCC's Public Safety and Homeland Security Bureau (Bureau) released its final report on the test. *See* Strengthening the Emergency Alert System (EAS): Lessons Learned from the Nationwide EAS Test, April 2013 (attached). The report describes the work of the FCC, the Federal Emergency Management Agency (FEMA) and other EAS stakeholders in planning and preparing for the test and summarizes the results of the test. As FCC representatives reported to GAO, the Bureau concludes that the November 9, 2011 test was generally successful in that it demonstrated that the national EAS, when activated, performs as designed. As expected, the test also uncovered several problems that impeded the ability of some EAS Participants to receive and/or retransmit the Emergency Action Notification (EAN) code, the code used to activate the national EAS. The Bureau's report includes several recommendations that will help to ensure that the EAS continues to serve as a reliable and effective method for the President as well as state and local governments to send timely and accurate emergency alerts to the American public.

The draft GAO report recommends that the Chairman of the FCC provide states with additional guidance (e.g., templates of EAS plan) to facilitate completion of updated state EAS plans that include Integrated Public Alert and Warning System (IPAWS)-compatible equipment. As discussed in its report, the Bureau has recommended that the Commission commence a rulemaking proceeding on state EAS plans as well as other issues. In addition, the Bureau has recommended that the Commission encourage State Emergency Communications Committees, the groups that typically develop state EAS plans, to review and update their current plans to ensure that they contain accurate EAS monitoring assignments. The FCC plans to take action to implement both of these recommendations in the near future.

The draft report also recommends that the Commission review and update its Wireless Emergency Alerts (WEA) (formerly known as Commercial Mobile Alert System (CMAS)) rules. The FCC plans to conduct such a review in the near future. As FCC representatives explained

during the exit interview and in the attached comments, the FCC plans to task its recently
rechartered Communications Security, Reliability and Interoperability Council (CSRIC) with
review of these rules and to recommend any changes to FCC rules as necessary. CSRIC is a
federal advisory committee comprised of representatives from Federal, state and local
governments, the communications industry and non-profit organizations and is tasked with
advising the FCC on actions it can take to ensure the security, reliability and interoperability of
communications systems, including public safety, telecommunications and media
communications. The FCC believes this approach is appropriate given the voluntary nature of
the program. Unlike EAS, where broadcasters and other EAS Participants are required to receive
and transmit national EAS alerts, under the Warning Alert and Response Network Act,
commercial wireless provider participation in WEA is voluntary. This means wireless carriers
can elect to participate in whole, in part or not at all. In addition, those carriers that originally
elected to participate may withdraw their participation. In light of this, the FCC's approach with
WEA has been to encourage government alert originators, FEMA, and the wireless industry to
develop consensus-based solutions for WEA. This is the approach the FCC took in adopting the
original rules in 2008. Under this approach, the FCC would first ask the CSRIC to conduct a
review and develop consensus-based recommendations for actions the Commission should take
to improve the WEA rules. The Commission can then consider those recommendations in
deciding appropriate action, including a Notice of Proposed Rulemaking. We believe this multi-
stakeholder approach will yield positive results that not only will encourage state and local
government alert originators to participate in FEMA's IPAWS, but also will encourage more
commercial wireless carriers, including those that are smaller or that serve rural communities, to
elect to participate in the program and send timely and accurate alerts to their subscribers.

Finally, the FCC looks forward to continuing its work with FEMA on outreach to state
and local government agencies and the public on IPAWS capabilities and to develop a strategy
for regular testing of the EAS. The FCC also will continue to support FEMA as it develops a
plan to disseminate national-level alerts via IPAWS.

Sincerely,

David S. Turetsky
Chief, Public Safety and Homeland
Security Bureau

2

Appendix V: GAO Contact and Staff Acknowledgments

GAO Contact	Mark Goldstein (202) 512-2834 or goldsteinm@gao.gov
Staff Acknowledgments	In addition to the individual named above, Sally Moino, Assistant Director; Andy Clinton; Jean Cook; Bert Japikse; Delwen Jones; Jennifer Kim; Josh Ormond; Carl Ramirez; Jerry Sandau; and Andrew Stavisky made key contributions to this report.

GAO's Mission	The Government Accountability Office, the audit, evaluation, and investigative arm of Congress, exists to support Congress in meeting its constitutional responsibilities and to help improve the performance and accountability of the federal government for the American people. GAO examines the use of public funds; evaluates federal programs and policies; and provides analyses, recommendations, and other assistance to help Congress make informed oversight, policy, and funding decisions. GAO's commitment to good government is reflected in its core values of accountability, integrity, and reliability.
Obtaining Copies of GAO Reports and Testimony	The fastest and easiest way to obtain copies of GAO documents at no cost is through GAO's website (http://www.gao.gov). Each weekday afternoon, GAO posts on its website newly released reports, testimony, and correspondence. To have GAO e-mail you a list of newly posted Products, go to http://www.gao.gov and select "E-mail Updates."
Order by Phone	The price of each GAO publication reflects GAO's actual cost of production and distribution and depends on the number of pages in the publication and whether the publication is printed in color or black and white. Pricing and ordering information is posted on GAO's website, http://www.gao.gov/ordering.htm. Place orders by calling (202) 512-6000, toll free (866) 801-7077, or TDD (202) 512-2537. Orders may be paid for using American Express, Discover Card, MasterCard, Visa, check, or money order. Call for additional information.
Connect with GAO	Connect with GAO on Facebook, Flickr, Twitter, and YouTube. Subscribe to our RSS Feeds or E-mail Updates. Listen to our Podcasts. Visit GAO on the web at www.gao.gov.
To Report Fraud, Waste, and Abuse in Federal Programs	Contact: Website: http://www.gao.gov/fraudnet/fraudnet.htm E-mail fraudnet@gao.gov Automated answering system: (800) 424-5454 or (202) 512-7470
Congressional Relations	Katherine Siggerud, Managing Director, siggerudk@gao.gov, (202) 512-4400, U.S. Government Accountability Office, 441 G Street NW, Room 7125, Washington, DC 20548
Public Affairs	Chuck Young, Managing Director, youngc1@gao.gov, (202) 512-4800 U.S. Government Accountability Office, 441 G Street NW, Room 7149 Washington, DC 20548

Please Print on Recycled Paper.